Aesop's Fables

The Goose That Laid the Golden Eggs
&
Other Fables

 Retold by Andrea Stacy Leach
Illustrated by Holly Hannon

Paradise Press, Inc.

The Fables

The Goose That Laid the Golden Eggs

$\mathcal{O}$nce upon a time, there was a poor farmer who owned a goose. He and his wife earned their living by selling the goose's eggs at the market. One day the farmer found an unusual egg in the goose's nest. He rushed home to show it to his wife.

"That egg is pure gold!" she cried. They hurried to the market and sold the egg. Then the farmer and his wife bought anything that caught their fancy. Soon they had no more money.

"We must check the goose's nest tomorrow to see if she lays another golden egg," the farmer said eagerly.

Sure enough, the next day—and every day after that—the goose laid a golden egg! No sooner were the eggs laid than the farmer and his wife were off to the market.

Eventually, the farmer became impatient. One day he said to his wife, "Why should we settle for just one egg each day? If I open up the goose, we can have all the gold at once!"

But when the farmer opened up the goose, he found no more golden eggs. Now the goose was dead, and the farmer and his wife were poor again, having spent all their money foolishly.

Those who want more than they have are often left with nothing.

The Mice in Council

The mice of the house were living in constant fear of their enemy, the cat. One day they called a meeting to decide how to handle the situation.

Many schemes were proposed and rejected. Finally a young mouse stood up and said, "Our problem is that we do not know when the cat is around. I propose we hang a bell around his neck to warn us when he is nearby."

The mice clapped and cheered, and they all agreed to the scheme.

Then the old mouse stood up and said, "This is a clever scheme. I have just one question. Who is going to bell the cat?"

Silence filled the room. Not one mouse was willing to take the risk of belling the cat.

It is one thing to propose, another to perform.

The Miller, His Son, and a Donkey

The miller and his son wanted to sell their donkey, and they set off for the village. On their way, some children began laughing at them. "Look at them walking beside the donkey. Why don't they ride it?"

So the miller put his son on the donkey. Soon they overtook a group of men arguing. One man shouted, "Look at that lazy boy riding while his father walks."

So the miller climbed on the donkey with his son.

They were nearing the village when a man saw them and said, "You there! Why do you put such a burden on that animal? You should be carrying him, not he carrying you."

The miller and his son, always eager to please, got off the donkey. They tied the donkey's legs together and carried the donkey on a pole. Everyone laughed at such a funny sight.

Frightened by the laughter, the donkey kicked free of the pole and ran away.

Try to please everyone
and you will
please no one.

The Crow and the Peacocks

One day the crow found some beautiful peacock feathers lying on the ground. He attached them to his small tail feathers and pretended to be a peacock.

"Why, I am as grand as any peacock," he thought. "Certainly too grand to stay with the crows!" And he hurried off to join the peacocks.

But the peacocks saw the crow for what he really was. They pecked at him until the peacock feathers fell off. The crow was lucky to escape with his own feathers!

When he returned to the crows, they said, "Don't expect us to be your friends. You had no time for us when you were a peacock." And they walked away, leaving the crow alone.

Never forget your proper identity.